The wonder of girls

"Innocence is the **first flower** of childhood"

"Make the most of every opportunity"

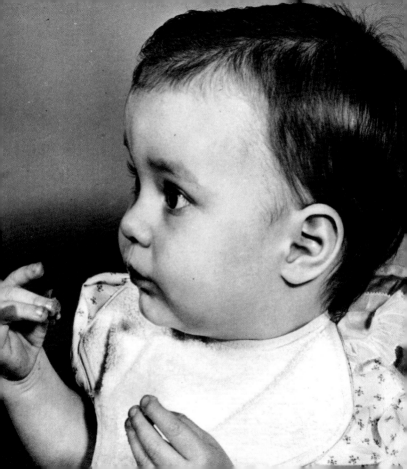

"What are **little girls** made of? What are **little girls** made of?"

"Sugar and spice and all things nice

– that's what little girls are made of..."

– Nursery rhyme

"...or at least that's the theory."

"Real girls are not afraid of the dark..."

"...they like adventure..."

"...and they **don't give up** when it all goes wrong!"

"There are **times** when **every** girl needs a **hand**"

"Some girls are gifted and clever..."

"but all girls can take that step forward"

"The knowingness of little girls..."

"...is hidden in their curls."

– Phillis McGinley

"Girls just want to have fun" – Cyndi Lauper